MW00872862

This Book Belongs To

_____

_____

_____

_____

_____

_____

_____

_____

_____

_____

_____

_____

_____

_____

_____

_____

_____

_____

_____

_____

_____

_____

_____

_____

_____

_____

AWESOME BIG BROTHER!

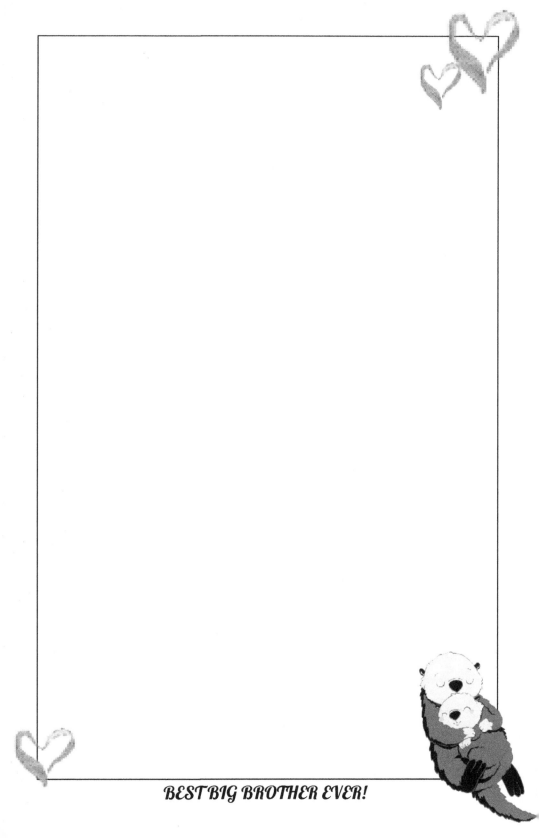

BEST BIG BROTHER EVER!

AWESOME BIG BROTHER!

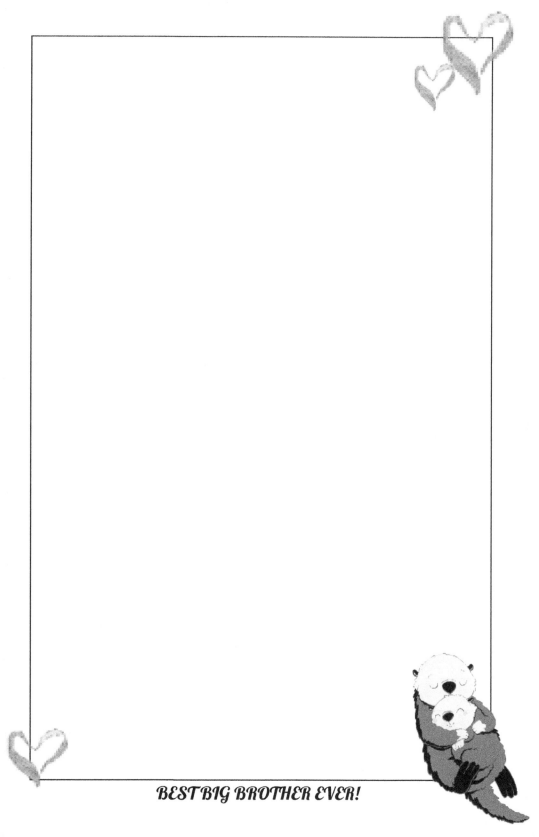

BEST BIG BROTHER EVER!

AWESOME BIG BROTHER!

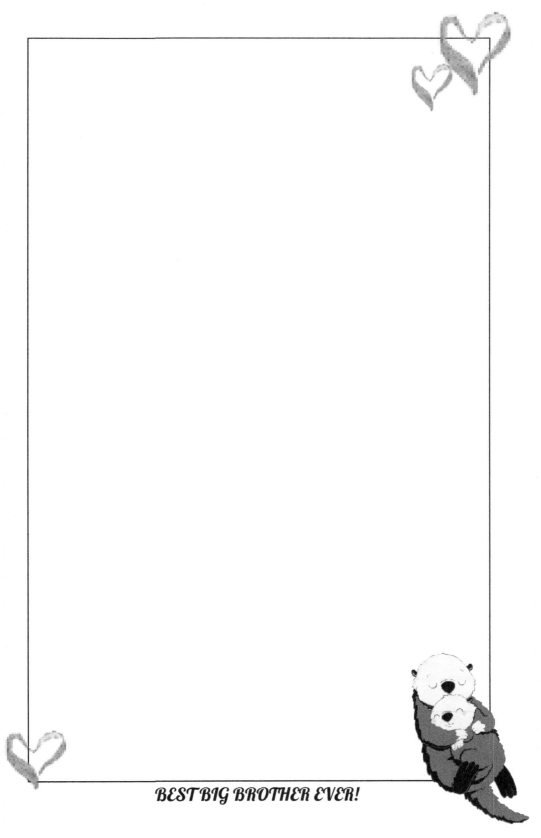

BEST BIG BROTHER EVER!

AWESOME BIG BROTHER!

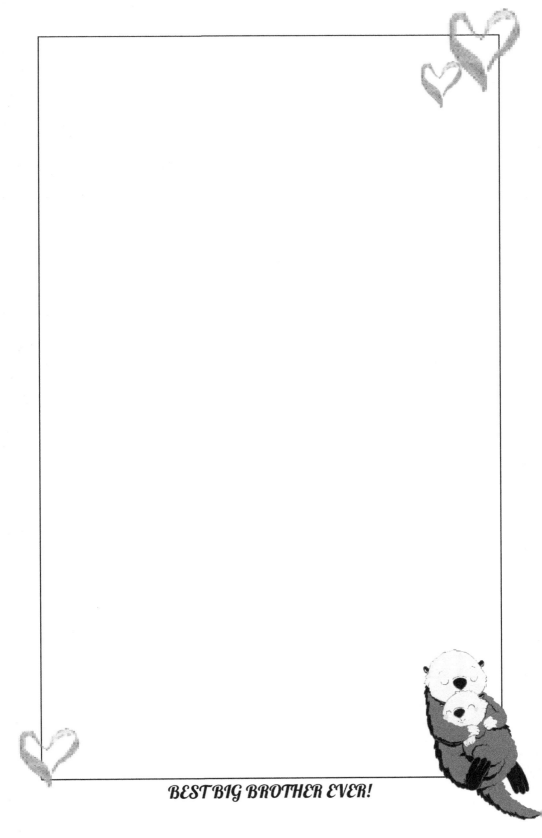

BEST BIG BROTHER EVER!

AWESOME BIG BROTHER!

BEST BIG BROTHER EVER!

AWESOME BIG BROTHER!

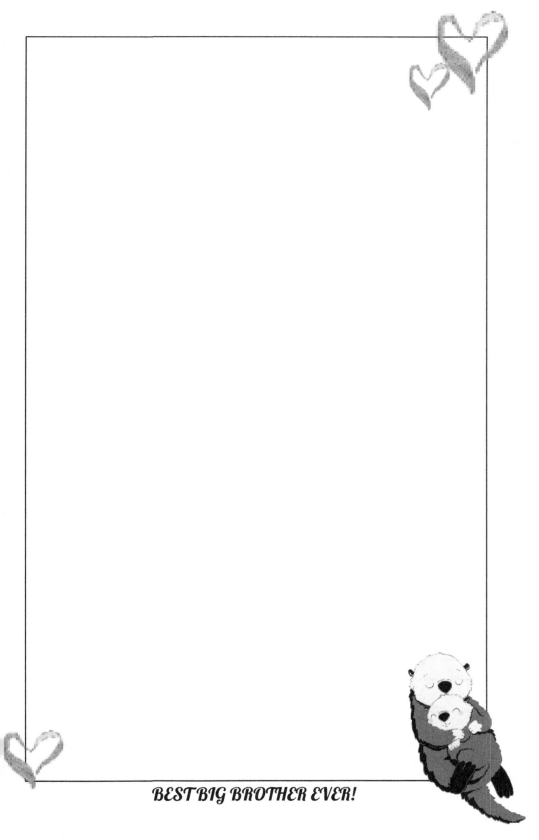

BEST BIG BROTHER EVER!

AWESOME BIG BROTHER!

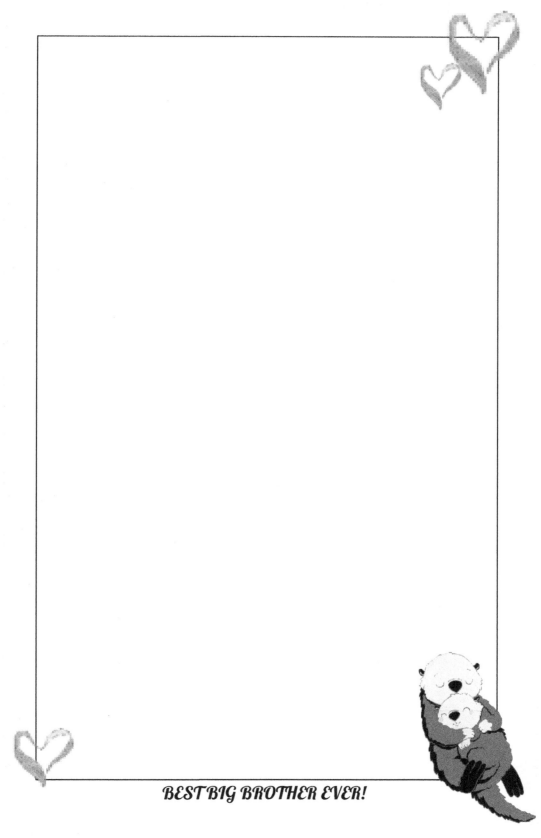

BEST BIG BROTHER EVER!

AWESOME BIG BROTHER!

BEST BIG BROTHER EVER!

_____

_____

_____

_____

_____

_____

_____

_____

_____

_____

_____

_____

_____

_____

_____

_____

_____

_____

_____

_____

_____

_____

_____

_____

_____

_____

AWESOME BIG BROTHER!

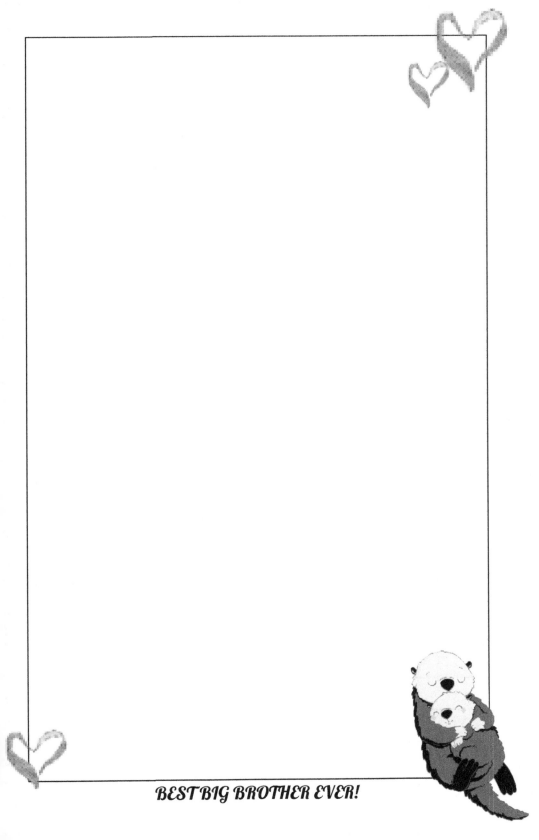

BEST BIG BROTHER EVER!

AWESOME BIG BROTHER!

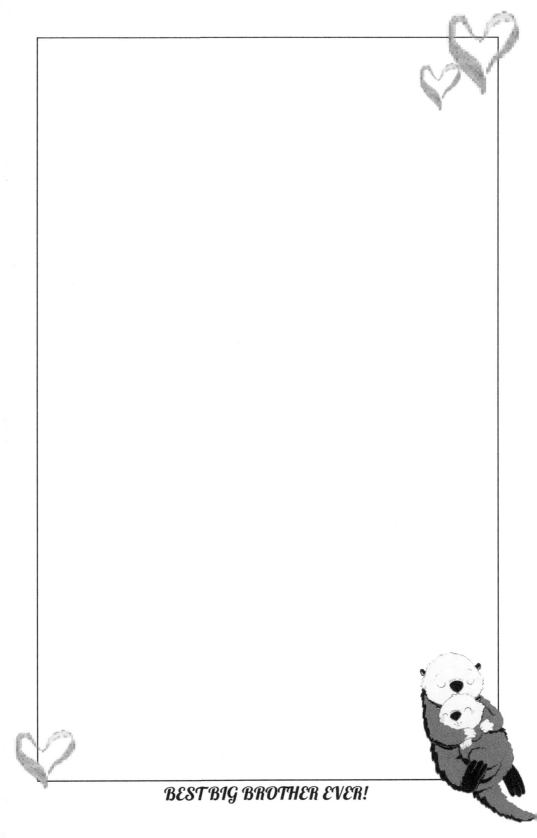

BEST BIG BROTHER EVER!

AWESOME BIG BROTHER!

BEST BIG BROTHER EVER!

_____

_____

_____

_____

_____

_____

_____

_____

_____

_____

_____

_____

_____

_____

_____

_____

_____

_____

_____

_____

_____

_____

_____

_____

_____

AWESOME BIG BROTHER!

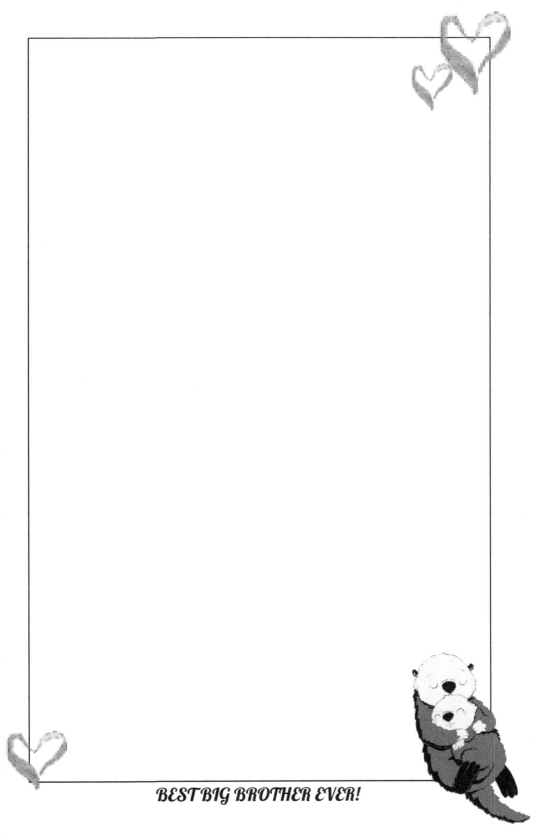

BEST BIG BROTHER EVER!

AWESOME BIG BROTHER!

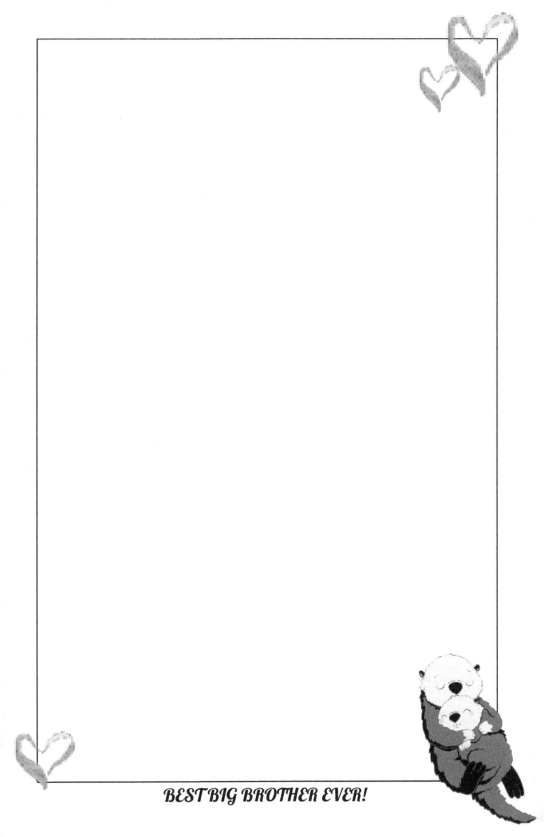

BEST BIG BROTHER EVER!

_____

_____

_____

_____

_____

_____

_____

_____

_____

_____

_____

_____

_____

_____

_____

_____

_____

_____

_____

_____

_____

_____

_____

_____

_____

_____

AWESOME BIG BROTHER!

BEST BIG BROTHER EVER!

_____

_____

_____

_____

_____

_____

_____

_____

_____

_____

_____

_____

_____

_____

_____

_____

_____

_____

_____

_____

_____

_____

_____

_____

_____

_____

AWESOME BIG BROTHER!

BEST BIG BROTHER EVER!

AWESOME BIG BROTHER!

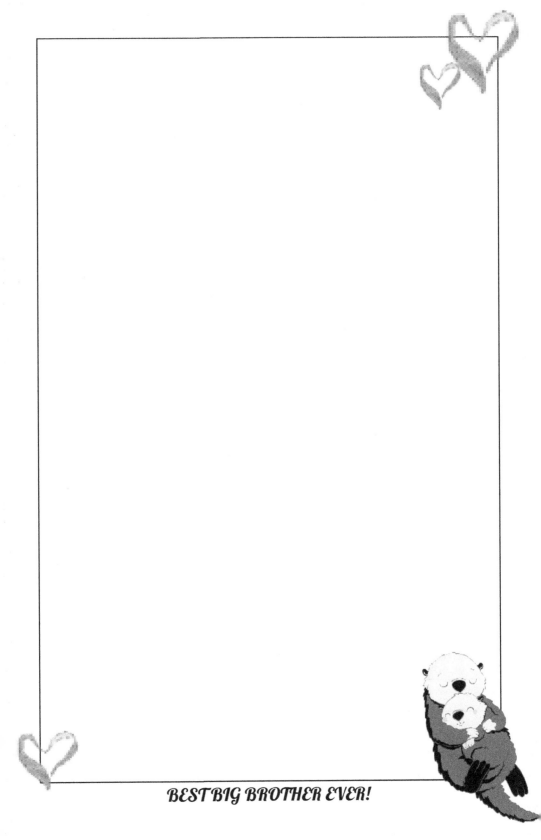

BEST BIG BROTHER EVER!

AWESOME BIG BROTHER!

BEST BIG BROTHER EVER!

AWESOME BIG BROTHER!

BEST BIG BROTHER EVER!

_____

_____
_____
_____
_____
_____
_____
_____
_____
_____
_____
_____
_____
_____
_____
_____
_____
_____
_____
_____
_____
_____
_____
_____

AWESOME BIG BROTHER!

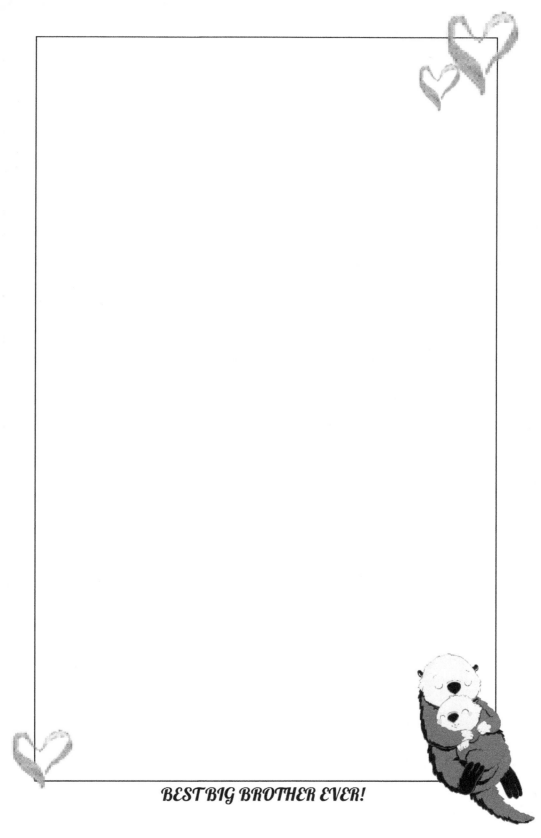

BEST BIG BROTHER EVER!

_____

_____

_____

_____

_____

_____

_____

_____

_____

_____

_____

_____

_____

_____

_____

_____

_____

_____

_____

_____

_____

_____

_____

AWESOME BIG BROTHER!

BEST BIG BROTHER EVER!

_____

_____

_____

_____

_____

_____

_____

_____

_____

_____

_____

_____

_____

_____

_____

_____

_____

_____

_____

_____

_____

_____

_____

_____

_____

_____

_____

_____

AWESOME BIG BROTHER!

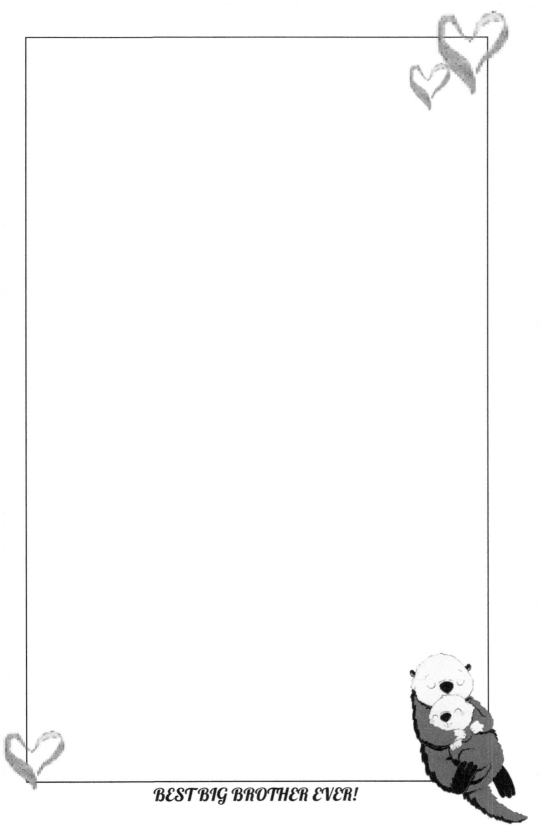

BEST BIG BROTHER EVER!

AWESOME BIG BROTHER!

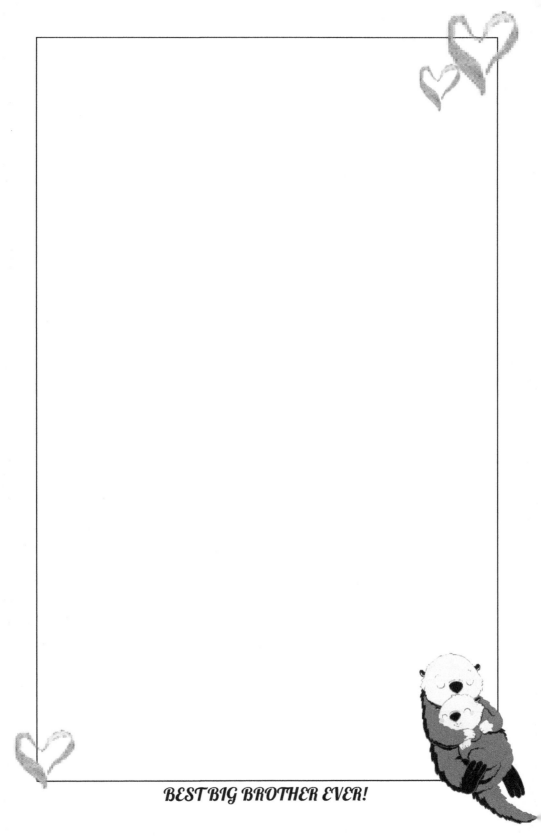

BEST BIG BROTHER EVER!

AWESOME BIG BROTHER!

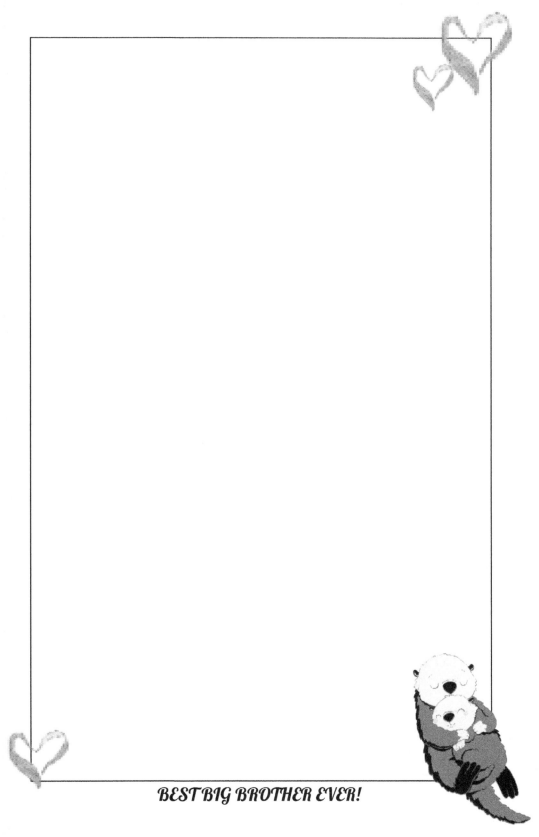

BEST BIG BROTHER EVER!

BEST BIG BROTHER EVER!

_____

_____

_____

_____

_____

_____

_____

_____

_____

_____

_____

_____

_____

_____

_____

_____

_____

_____

_____

_____

_____

_____

_____

_____

AWESOME BIG BROTHER!

BEST BIG BROTHER EVER!

AWESOME BIG BROTHER!

BEST BIG BROTHER EVER!

AWESOME BIG BROTHER!

BEST BIG BROTHER EVER!

AWESOME BIG BROTHER!

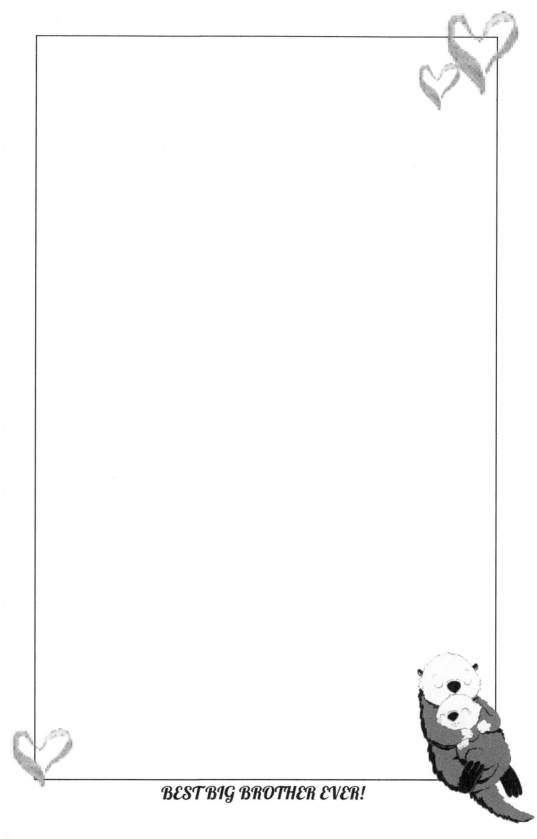

BEST BIG BROTHER EVER!

AWESOME BIG BROTHER!

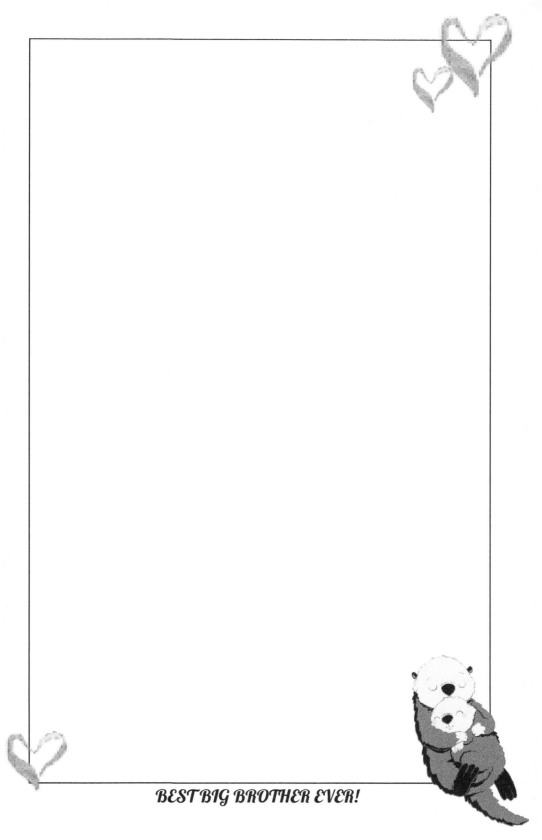

BEST BIG BROTHER EVER!

AWESOME BIG BROTHER!

BEST BIG BROTHER EVER!

AWESOME BIG BROTHER!

BEST BIG BROTHER EVER!

AWESOME BIG BROTHER!

BEST BIG BROTHER EVER!

_____

_____

_____

_____

_____

_____

_____

_____

_____

_____

_____

_____

_____

_____

_____

_____

_____

_____

_____

_____

_____

_____

_____

_____

AWESOME BIG BROTHER!

BEST BIG BROTHER EVER!

AWESOME BIG BROTHER!

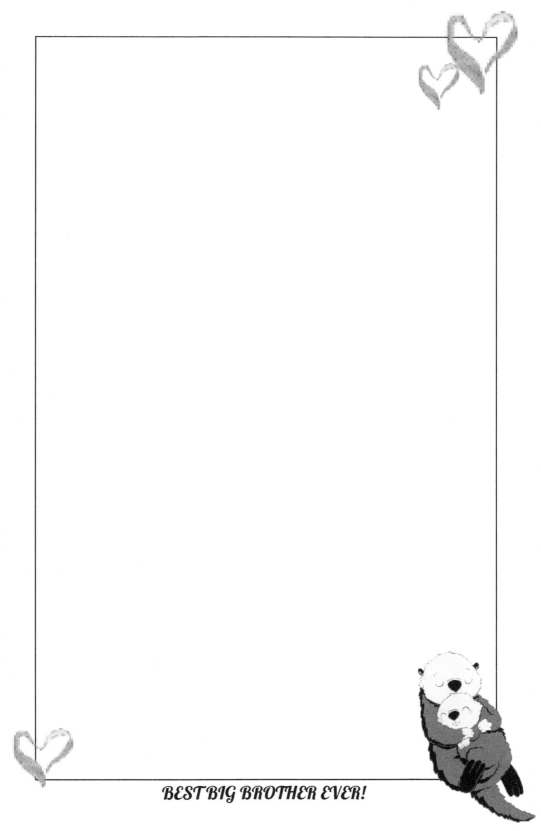

BEST BIG BROTHER EVER!

_____

_____

_____

_____

_____

_____

_____

_____

_____

_____

_____

_____

_____

_____

_____

_____

_____

_____

_____

_____

_____

_____

_____

_____

_____

_____

AWESOME BIG BROTHER!

BEST BIG BROTHER EVER!

AWESOME BIG BROTHER!

BEST BIG BROTHER EVER!

_____

_____

_____

_____

_____

_____

_____

_____

_____

_____

_____

_____

_____

_____

_____

_____

_____

_____

_____

_____

_____

_____

_____

AWESOME BIG BROTHER!

BEST BIG BROTHER EVER!

AWESOME BIG BROTHER!

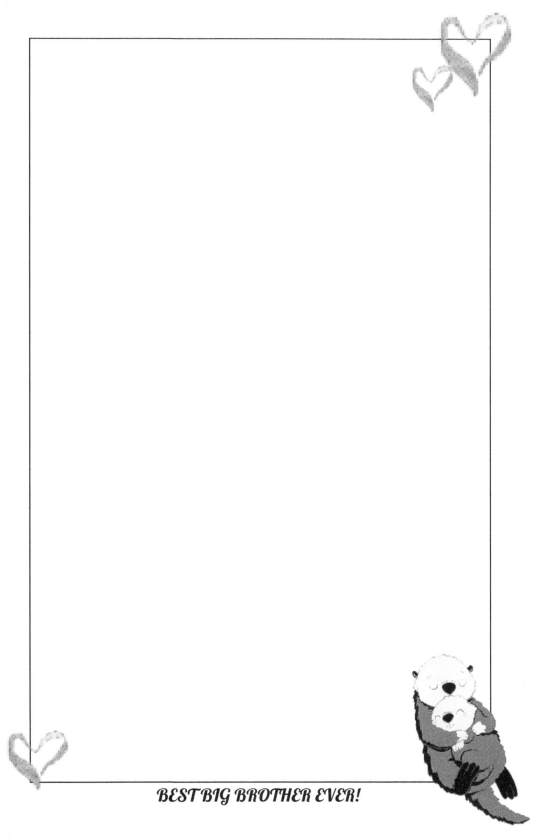

BEST BIG BROTHER EVER!

AWESOME BIG BROTHER!

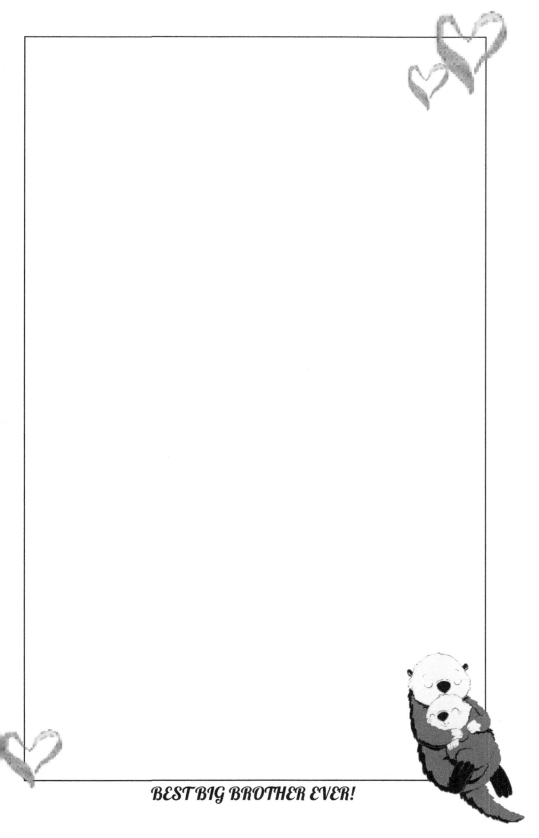

BEST BIG BROTHER EVER!

AWESOME BIG BROTHER!

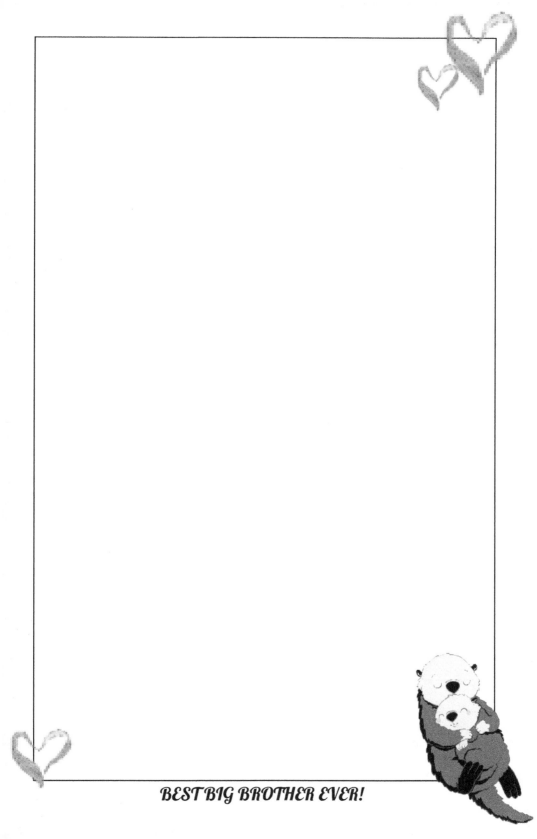

BEST BIG BROTHER EVER!

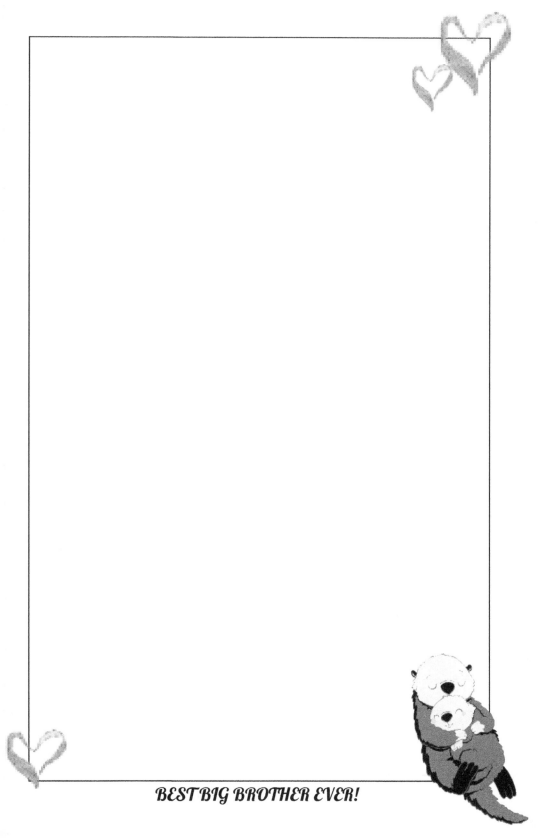

BEST BIG BROTHER EVER!

_____

_____

_____

_____

_____

_____

_____

_____

_____

_____

_____

_____

_____

_____

_____

_____

_____

_____

_____

_____

_____

_____

_____

_____

_____

_____

AWESOME BIG BROTHER!

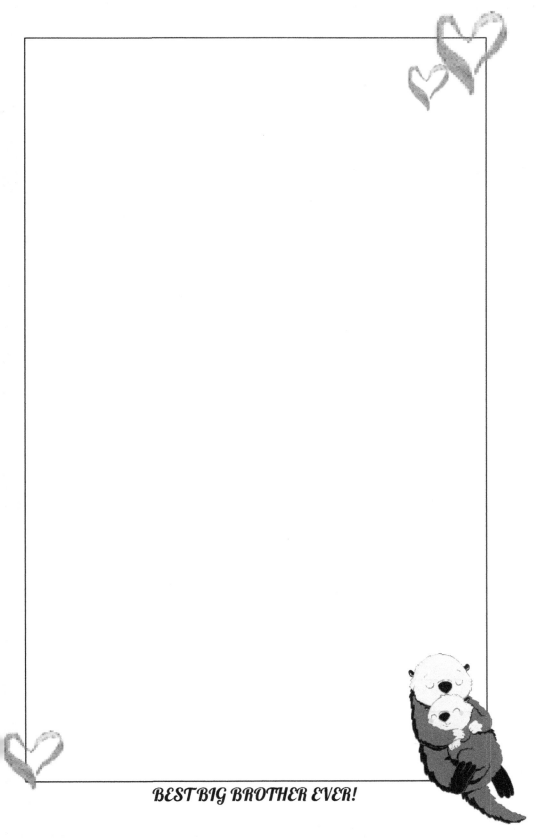

BEST BIG BROTHER EVER!

AWESOME BIG BROTHER!

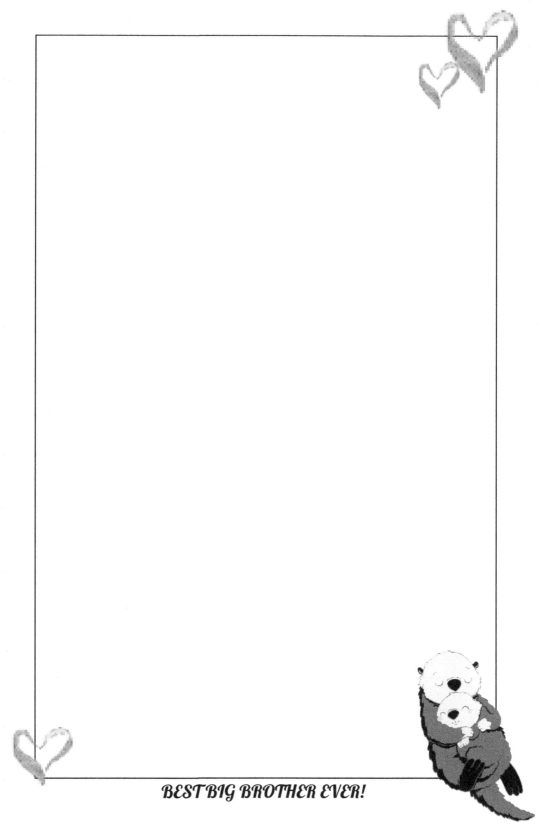

BEST BIG BROTHER EVER!

_____

_____

_____

_____

_____

_____

_____

_____

_____

_____

_____

_____

_____

_____

_____

_____

_____

_____

_____

_____

_____

_____

_____

AWESOME BIG BROTHER!

BEST BIG BROTHER EVER!

AWESOME BIG BROTHER!

BEST BIG BROTHER EVER!

AWESOME BIG BROTHER!

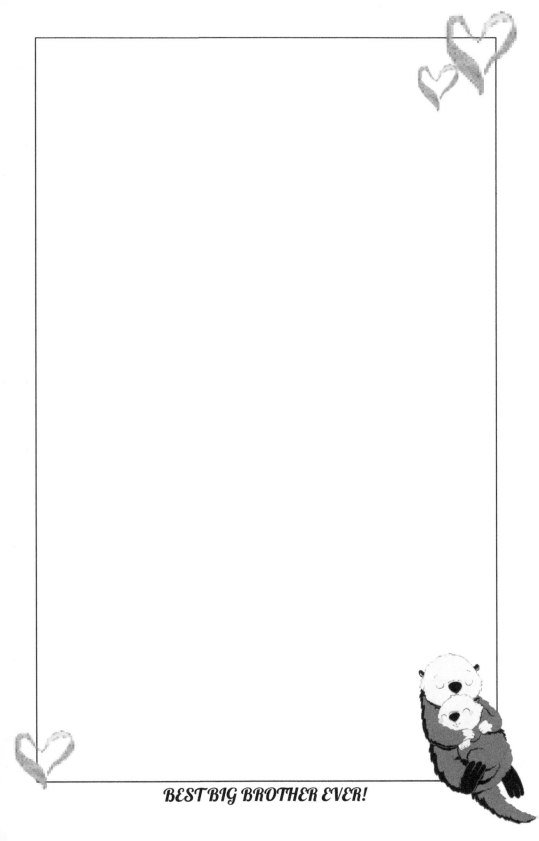

BEST BIG BROTHER EVER!

_____

_____
_____
_____
_____
_____
_____
_____
_____
_____
_____
_____
_____
_____
_____
_____
_____
_____
_____
_____
_____
_____
_____

AWESOME BIG BROTHER!

BEST BIG BROTHER EVER!

_____

_____

_____

_____

_____

_____

_____

_____

_____

_____

_____

_____

_____

_____

_____

_____

_____

_____

_____

_____

_____

_____

_____

_____

AWESOME BIG BROTHER!

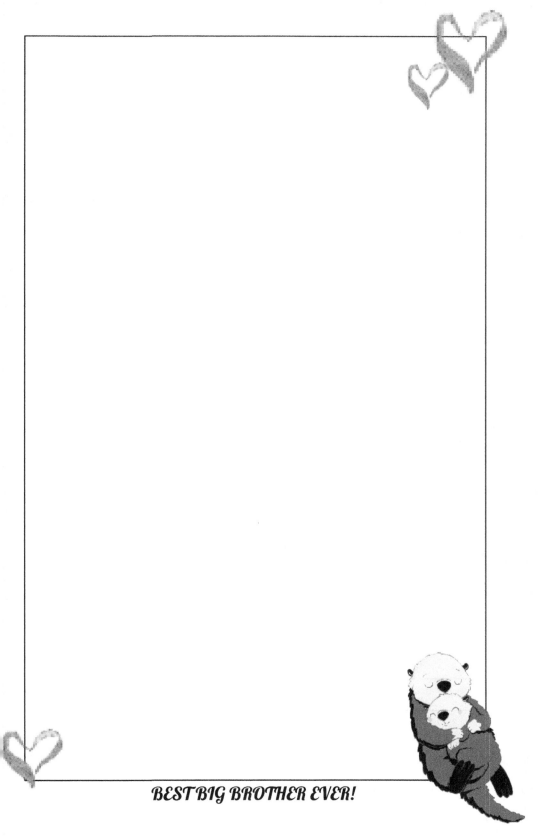

BEST BIG BROTHER EVER!

AWESOME BIG BROTHER!

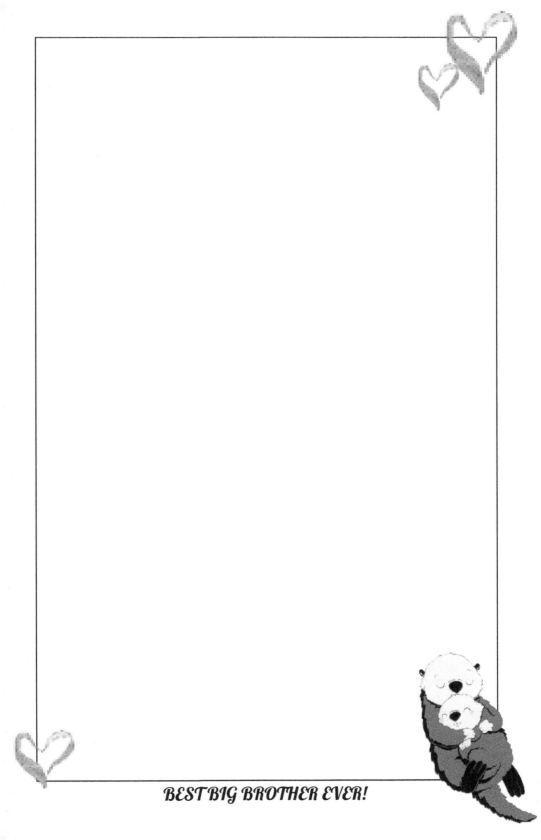

BEST BIG BROTHER EVER!

_____

_____

_____

_____

_____

_____

_____

_____

_____

_____

_____

_____

_____

_____

_____

_____

_____

_____

_____

_____

_____

_____

_____

_____

AWESOME BIG BROTHER!

BEST BIG BROTHER EVER!

AWESOME BIG BROTHER!

BEST BIG BROTHER EVER!

AWESOME BIG BROTHER!

BEST BIG BROTHER EVER!

_____

AWESOME BIG BROTHER!

BEST BIG BROTHER EVER!

_____

_____

_____

_____

_____

_____

_____

_____

_____

_____

_____

_____

_____

_____

_____

_____

_____

_____

_____

_____

_____

_____

AWESOME BIG BROTHER!

BEST BIG BROTHER EVER!

Made in United States
North Haven, CT
09 February 2024

48578441R00065